4.25

Published by ViVa Books

PO Box 28510, Kensington 2101, South Africa

First impression 1993
Reprinted 1995
Reprinted 1996

Original published in Expression (Lesotho), 1970

Cover illustration by Lois Head

Cover border and cover colour by Gillian Conry-Taylor

Photograph of Njabulo S Ndebele by Rashid Lombard

ISBN 1 874932 01 8

Reproduction by Remata Bureau and Printers

Printed and bound by Galvin & Sales, Cape Town
(1696)

Sarah, Rings and I

by Njabulo S Ndebele

Adapted by Ivan Vladislavić

Illustrated by Lois Head

BOOKS

Johannesburg

The Mystery of the Rings

There was something I could not understand about Sarah. Why did she have so many rings on her fingers? Who were the lucky men?

One morning Sarah and I were late for school. Teacher was guarding the gate and he caught us. He gave us six cuts each on the palms of our hands with his cane. This cane had a name: it was called Big Boy.

Teacher gave Sarah extra cuts because she was wearing so many rings. He made her take off the rings and he threw them into the drain.

I cried when Teacher hit me. Sarah did not cry, although her hand was red. I loved Sarah. So I hated Teacher because Sarah had seen me crying.

People said afterwards that Sarah took revenge on Teacher. The next day Teacher came to school with a white bandage around his head. Sarah had new rings on her fingers.

People said that Sarah asked some men to attack Teacher. I felt sorry for Teacher when he was

bandaged. He looked so sad. Sarah's men beat
him up badly. There were so many rings on
Sarah's fingers - one ring from each of her men.

A Resolution

The last day of school came. We filed like miners into the big, hot school hall to hear our examination results. This happened every year in December when the school closed.

This year I had made a resolution. I had decided to tell Sarah that I loved her. I would gaze into her eyes and say, 'Do you remember what we learned during Scripture lessons? We learned that the Bible says: "Love one another." Therefore, let us love one another, Sarah.'

Sarah would tell me that I was too young. She was five years older than I was. But that would not matter. People who were in love thought only about love. Sarah went out with so many big boys, and I would have no chance against them. But I would tell Sarah I loved her. I was afraid of Sarah. I was even afraid to greet her. But it was the end of the year and I had made up my mind.

We were only in Standard Three, and so our class was called 'The Babies'. We came into the hall first and sat on the front benches. It was hot in there.

My friend Doksi sat next to me and we both stared at the door. We wanted to see Sarah and her friend Tshidi come in. Doksi was in love with Tshidi, who was a very tall girl. She was two yards tall (or so people said).

Sarah and Tshidi were in Standard Six, and so they came in last. We envied the Standard Sixes. They were the brainy ones of the school. They used big words like 'corporal punishment' and 'abolished' in debates.

I remembered that one day during a debate Doksi tried to be clever. He put up his hand to speak. The brainy ones jeered at him and he began to cry loudly.

Then I said to Doksi, 'I told you to be quiet! I told you!'

Doksi cried more. The chairman of the debate ordered him to go and cry outside. Two big boys carried Doksi out into the street. People said that Doksi cried all the way home. But he said it wasn't true.

But now I saw Sarah come in. I hoped more than ever that I had passed. Then she would see how clever I was.

'Where are they?' Doksi asked.

'Didn't you see them?' I asked back.

'I did, but then I lost them in the crowd.'

'It's your own fault then.' Doksi liked to cry. But before he could start crying, I went on, 'I'll stand up as if I'm tightening my belt. Then I'll look to see where they are.' He nodded.

When I stood up, I saw Sarah and Tshidi at the back of the hall. They were standing with some other girls on top of a table. I sat down again. 'They are standing on a table,' I reported.

'Where?' Doksi nudged me with his bandaged elbow. Doksi had fallen from a tree while we were playing Tarzan, along with Wibbie, Lincoln and Monna. The five of us once saw a film about Tarzan, the King of the Apes. After that, we always tried to swing on branches the way Tarzan did. We laughed at Doksi when he fell and hurt his elbow. We said he had fallen like a bag of potatoes. Doksi cried.

'Where man?' Doksi asked again.

'At the back,' I said crossly. He was annoying me with his questions.

Doksi stood up as if he was loosening his belt and looked. Then he sat down with a broad smile on his face. He patted me on the shoulder. That annoyed me even more.

Then Doksi said sadly, 'I feel mad when I think that Tshidi is in love with my brother. *Nx!* He is only a factory worker.'

I knew how Doksi felt. Every Sunday afternoon I saw Sarah holding hands with a different big boy. That made me feel mad too.

'Here are your results!' bellowed Teacher. He was the one who had been ambushed by Sarah's men. He still had the scars on his forehead. 'First, the Babie-e-e-s ...'

Teacher yawned. He did not cover his mouth with his hand when he yawned. Doksi and I laughed. Teacher went on speaking.

'... then the Fours, the Fives, and lastly, the Sixes.'

It was hot and quiet in the hall. What if I had failed? Mother always told me to study hard, but I didn't listen to her.

'Now we will find out who has been playing with Satan instead of learning,' Teacher said. 'All the failures will go to hell.'

That made us grumble. It was hot and tense in the hall. Doksi looked at me. His lips trembled. I was afraid he would cry, but he did not.

'Shut up, monkeys!' shouted Teacher. He waved Big Boy in the air. There was silence at once. Everybody was afraid of Big Boy.

'Now listen. Those who have passed are as follows: John Radebe, Samuel Hlatshwayo, Visie Nkosi, Samuel Zwane ...'

What would happen to me if I failed? I
wondered. I would go to hell. Hell!

'... Judith Sibeko, Carolina Maduna, Lincoln
Nkosi, Deborah Mashinini, Daniel Zwane-e-e ...'

Teacher yawned again. A fly buzzed around his
head. He threatened it with Big Boy, but the fly
was not afraid of the cane. Then Teacher spotted
an old exercise book on the
floor. He picked it up and
flung it angrily at the fly.
The fly flew away to
safety.

The Principal chuckled. We thought that if the Principal laughed, then we pupils were also allowed to laugh. We all laughed merrily.

'SHUT YOUR BEAKS!' Teacher yelled.

We shut our beaks. The Principal shut his beak too.

'Sibusiso Twala,' continued Teacher, 'Penise Sibeko, Doksi Mbewe ...'

So Doksi had passed. Then I was sure that I would pass as well. I always beat Doksi in class. Of course, it made him cry.

'... Rogers Vilakazi, Agnes Maphanga, Emily Mahlangu, Jabu Mahaye ...'

That was me! I had passed! Everyone had heard my name read out. Even Sarah. If only I could speak to her. I would tell her what the Bible said: 'Love one another.' Then I would add that I had passed my exams. My grandfather once said I would become a famous man. I would tell Sarah that too ...

Sarah passed, but she did not do well. I suppose she was more interested in rings than in studying. She had so many rings!

Home Sweet Home!

When Teacher finished reading out the results, we sang 'Our Father'. Then we sang *'Nkosi Sikelel' iAfrika'*.

And finally we sang *'Die Stem'*. We didn't know the words of this song, so we just chattered like monkeys in tune with the music.

We poured noisily out of the hall. Some of us were sulking, others were dancing with joy. Those who had passed mocked those who had failed. Doksi and I lost Sarah and Tshidi in the confusion. I laughed at Doksi because his girl had failed.

'Where is she?' Doksi asked.

'Where are *they*?' I replied angrily.

'I don't know,' he replied. 'I lost them in the crowd.'

I could hardly hear Doksi. All around us the children were singing 'Home Sweet Home'. 'Let's look for them,' I shouted. 'Today is the day!'

Then we began to fight our way through the crowd of singing children. I was sure that Sarah was watching this act of bravery.

'ZING ZING TARZAN!' Doksi yelled. 'TARZAN THE APEMAN! ZING ZING!'

Doksi always became mad when he played Tarzan. We fought our way through the children like Tarzan finding a path through the jungle. Many of the girls smelt like *magwinya*. Some of them had lots of Vaseline on their faces and they were brown with dust. 'ZING ZING!' Doksi yelled. He did not worry about his sore elbow. He was brave. And he did not worry about the smell of *magwinya*. Crocodiles smell much worse.

I followed right behind Tarzan, until he stopped suddenly and shouted, 'There they are!' Sarah and Tshidi were standing with two boys. They were laughing at jokes we couldn't hear.

'Let's go to them,' Doksi said.

I wanted to, but somehow my legs became heavy.

'Come on, let's go,' Doksi said. 'What's wrong with you?'

My legs became heavier. My mouth was dry.

'Are you a coward? OK, I'll tell her that you love her.'

'No! Don't do that!'

'Then what are you waiting for? Let's go.'

My legs were very heavy. My mouth was so dry that it was painful when I swallowed.

'You're a coward,' Doksi said. 'You are afraid of a girl. I am going to tell the others, and we will all laugh at you. Eh! I shall tell them that Jabu is afraid of a girl.'

I tried to speak, but the words would not come out. In my head I heard myself saying, *'OK, Doksi, let's go. But I'm afraid. I love Sarah. But I'm afraid.'*

But Doksi didn't hear me. Only I could hear this little voice in my head. The voice said, *'I'm afraid. Sarah is five years older than I am! Can't your thick eyes see?'*

'Here I go,' Doksi said. 'I'll tell her that you love her.'

'Wait!' Still the words would not come out. My voice hurt my dry throat when I tried to speak. Doksi was going to tell them that I was a

coward. They would laugh at me. They would laugh at me until I cried. They would laugh at me for a whole week when we played soccer in the afternoon. *'Wait! Wait!'*

But Doksi did not wait. I watched him walk towards Sarah. Then I wished I had two glasses of Coca-Cola. I would go up to Sarah and give her one. That is what men did in films. Sarah and I would raise our glasses and clink them together. Then we would drink ...

Doksi spoke to Sarah and her friends, and they all laughed. Aw! I thought, Doksi has made a joke about me! Tshidi patted Doksi's shoulder. She was twice as tall as him. She bent down

from high above and kissed him on the
forehead. Aw! I thought, Doksi has won.

Then Doksi spoke again and they all turned
towards me. Doksi pointed at me.

Somehow my throat had become wet. 'Home
Sweet Home!' I shouted, and my voice came out
loud and clear. Somehow my legs had become
very light. I turned sharply on my heel. I was
soon lost in crowds of children who smelt of
magwinya and *atjar*.

As I hurried along, I thought about what Doksi
had done. Doksi had told Tshidi that he loved

her. She had kissed him. He had also told Sarah about me. He would boast about it, and offer to teach me how to become brave.

'I'll give Tshidi my handkerchiefs to wash,' Doksi would say, 'and she'll bring them back smelling of sweet powder!' How he would boast! 'I twisted her hand until she agreed to be my girl,' Doksi would say.

Anyway, Sarah was five years older than I, and she had so many rings on her fingers. But I loved Sarah. How Doksi would boast! I wouldn't stand for it!

Another One!

We scattered into the street. Many children were dancing and running and singing and throwing orange-peels at one another. Some were laughing at those who had failed.

Some boys were telling girls that they loved them. They twisted the girls' arms until they accepted their love. Other boys were going to Mamba Stadium to fight. The boys had put these fights off until closing-day.

A lot of girls stood in the road when cars came.
When the cars hooted, the girls pretended to get
a fright and jumped out of the way. They lifted
their dresses behind and showed us their
panties. But when Baba Ngwenya's taxi came
the girls all ran away, because Baba Ngwenya
had a *sjambok*.

Then it happened.

As I ran into the street, something hit me in the
eye. It was a ball of paper. Someone had
chewed the paper, and it was wet with spit. The
ball broke into small pieces, which went all over
my face.

'*Sies!* Your mother's bottom!' I cursed, wiping
my face. Everyone laughed.

'Hhe-e-yi! They got him!'

'You blasted him well!'

'He is too proud!'

'Just because they have a street at his home!'

'They eat sandwiches at his home!'

'Throw another one at him!'

'That's right! Throw another one!'

They began to chant: 'Another one! Another one! Another one!'

It is all my father's fault, I thought. They are teasing me because he is Principal of the High School. And because the street where we live is named after him. Why did Father let the council name a street after him? It wasn't fair.

Just then Sarah, Tshidi, the two big boys and Doksi came around the corner. Let them come! I would show Sarah I was brave.

'Come out!' I demanded. 'Whoever threw that ball, come out!'

But the chant drowned out my voice. Then my
throat began to dry up again. And my voice
hurt my throat when I tried to speak.

'Throw another one at him!' the crowd called.
'Another one! Another one! He thinks he is
clever.'

The chant seemed to make them mad. They
closed in on me. I stood on guard. I had to
show Sarah I was brave. 'Come out!' I
demanded. 'Let the man who did it come out!'

But my throat hurt. My voice became softer and
softer, until no one could hear it. But I could still
hear it in my head. *'Let him come out,'* this small
voice said bravely. *'Let him come, and I shall hit
him until he calls his brothers. Let him call his whole
family. I shall chase them all away with six blows of
my fist.'*

My throat hurt. They did not hear me. They
were still chanting, and it made them even
madder. They closed in on me. Many hands
grabbed me. They were mad. *'Come out!'* They
were mad. They threw me up into the air. They
danced about with me. They bounced me like a

ball from one pair of hands to another. I saw
Sarah and her friends pointing at me and
laughing.

Then Doksi too thought that he was brave. He
ran to help me, and called out, 'Come one, come
all!' He was just like a pirate attacking a ship.
But he was also lifted into the air. They danced
about with us. Doksi began to cry. At least I
was not crying. I'm sure Sarah saw that I was
not crying.

At last the mad children got tired. They put us
down at Twala's Butchery, opposite the school.
They scattered like chickens do when a car
comes. Some of the girls lifted their dresses
behind. Doksi threw a stone at one of them and
hit her on the bottom. She cried with pain as
they all ran away.

Doksi said he would remember them all. We would ambush them in the evenings when they were sent to the shops.

'What happened?' Doksi asked, wiping away his tears.

'They lifted me into the air. Didn't you see, stupid?'

'Yes, I saw them lifting you up and I ran to help you.'

'Oho! You were no help at all.'

'I would have rescued you,' said Doksi. 'But my elbow is wounded.'

'You are no friend of mine. Why did you tell Sarah that I love her? Hey?'

'I didn't,' said Doksi, beginning to cry again.

'What happened then?'

'I just told them you were my friend,' Doksi said, sniffing. 'And then Tshidi gave me a message for my brother.'

'What message?'

'She wants my brother to take her to the bioscope tonight.'

'Well, did you tell Tshidi you love her, Tarzan?'

'No. Those two gorillas kept on grabbing the girls. After they gave me the message, they forgot about me.'

That reminded me of Sarah and Tshidi. I saw them walking two-for-two down the old tar road. They were holding hands with their gorillas.

'Let us throw stones at them,' I suggested. 'I hate those gorillas!'

But Doksi just said, '*Nx!*'

So I decided to teach Sarah's gorilla a lesson. I shot him down with my Luger pistol. I was just like a German spy.

I rode over him with my Mercedes Benz convertible to make sure he was dead. Then Sarah and I climbed into my Benza-Benza. We sailed over the sea, and we flew into the sky. I bought her everything she wanted from my shops over the clouds. Then each of my six aeroplanes brought us a child. Sarah and I and our beautiful children lived happily ever after ...

Anyway, that's what I imagined ...

A Conversation

Doksi decided to go home. He said he was not going to give his brother the message from Tshidi. Instead, he had a brilliant idea: he would tell Tshidi that his brother was ill. He would take Tshidi to the bioscope in his brother's place. I envied Doksi.

I started to walk home. I soon caught up with Sarah and the others. As I was passing them a little girl said, 'Here's the child who was hit in the eye with a big ball!'

Sarah laughed. Tshidi laughed too. Even the gorillas made croaking noises. I was angry. I threw a stone at the girl who had made Sarah laugh at me. It hit her on the head, and she ran away crying. I waved my fist at her.

'Heyi wena!' a girl shouted behind me. *'Heyi wena!'*

I turned around. It was Sarah! She was coming towards me. Then my legs became heavy again. Many thoughts raced through my mind. No! I couldn't tell Sarah I loved her. I was not ready for that. I couldn't twist her hand. Everybody was watching. Sarah had too many rings on her fingers. Sarah knew lots of men. Besides, she was five years older than I was. I was afraid of Sarah's men. If they took their revenge on me, I would have to bandage my head like Teacher. Sarah was coming towards me.

'No, Sarah,' I thought, *'don't come to me!'*

But my mind was still racing. Sarah was coming to me. I didn't want Sarah any more. But I loved her! Sarah was coming to me. Closer and closer. She stopped a short distance away. I looked at my toes.

'Come here, *Baba*,' Sarah said.

But my legs were so heavy I could not move.

'Why do the other children worry you so much?' Sarah asked.

I did not answer. My throat hurt a little.

'Shame!' Sarah said with a smile. 'What do you want with me? You are always looking at me.'

Somehow her smile brought my voice back. '*Hhayi!*' I burst out. 'I have never looked at you.' But when I said that, I felt hot all over with embarrassment.

'This child!' she exclaimed, clapping her hands. 'You are telling a lie.'

'I just like to look at you,' I admitted.

'I also like to look at you,' Sarah laughed. 'But you are still a baby.'

'What if I were old?' I was feeling braver. My throat did not hurt any more.

'Hha! You're silly. This child!'

'True's God, I'm not silly.'

'Where is Teboho?' Sarah asked. Teboho was my sister.

'I don't know,' I replied. 'I suppose she is at home.'

'Tell her I shall come to see her this evening.'

I nodded. I was overjoyed. Sarah would be coming to my house.

'Do you know my name?' she asked.

'Sarah!'

'Hawu! This child knows me.'

I grinned mysteriously. Then I looked down
and drew a funny person in the sand with my
big toe ...

Waiting for Sarah

I arrived home at half past four. My dog Danger
came running to meet me.

Mother was not home, because she was working
late today. Teboho was nowhere to be seen
either, although Mother had asked her to come
straight home after school.

I played with Danger for a while, throwing a
tennis-ball for him. But he soon became bored

with the game. I went inside and began to clean the house. Mother would be very pleased to find the house clean when she came from work.

I did everything that Miss Shezi had taught us during Hygiene. I dusted the furniture. Then I washed all the pots and dishes in the kitchen. I even wiped the 'Ellis Deluxe' stove.

I put my exercise book on the table in the sitting-room. I opened it to a test in which I had scored ten out of ten. I tore out the test in which I had scored three out of twenty. When Sarah came, she would see that I was not a silly child.

It grew dark. Teboho still did not come home. I sat down on the sofa to wait. Perhaps Teboho had gone to church for hymn practice? I thought. The choir always practised at seven on Friday evenings.

I began to hope that Teboho would stay away.
Sarah would come soon. Then the two of us
would be alone together. I would offer to take
Sarah to the church. It would be nice to walk in
the dark with Sarah.

I remembered what Sarah had said to me after
school. She had said, 'Come here, *Baba*.' Yes,
she had called me *Baba*. Mother sometimes
called Father *Baba*. Perhaps Sarah loved me?
Mother certainly loved Father.

I was glad that Doksi and I had heard Miss Shezi
and Teacher talking about love. It happened one
night after a concert at the school. Miss Shezi
and Teacher went into the bushes behind the
school hall. Doksi and I tied our handkerchiefs
over our mouths, like robbers in a film. Then we
sneaked after them and hid behind a rock.

'There are two important kinds of kisses,'
Teacher said. 'They are the English kiss and the
French kiss. Which one do you prefer?'

'The nicer one,' Miss Shezi said.

'Well, the nicer one is the French kiss,' Teacher

explained. 'But it is only done when people are in bed.'

'Then we should rather do the English kiss,' Miss Shezi suggested.

Then they did it. They kissed. Doksi and I saw them clearly. If Sarah loved me, I would hold her tightly. I would hum a little in her ear. Then I would put out my tongue. Sarah would open her mouth and let my tongue in. We would kiss for ten minutes on end, just like Teacher said.

At that moment I heard footsteps outside. Danger began to bark. Then a voice called, 'Teboho!' It was Sarah! Sarah was coming!

The Kiss

Sarah and I went walking in the dark ...

I closed the front gate carefully so that Danger could not follow us.

We went along the street that was named after my father. We passed the old Jew's shop. Then we crossed the tar road, which was lined with lights. This road went to town, to Johannesburg and Springs, and far away.

We went across the golf-course. It was very dark there. There were many anthills and molehills. We had to be careful not to trip over them. Teboho used to mock the golf-course. She called it the City of Anthills. 'How on earth do people manage to play golf on such a course?' she would say.

Sometimes Doksi, S'manga, Monna, Wibbie and I would trap the moles. We took them to Mavimbela the *inyanga*. He would give us five shillings for them. Then we bought fish and chips from the Jew's shop.

In the summer we trapped birds at the golf-course. The golfers chased us away with their clubs. Sometimes we left our birds behind in the panic and the golfers set them free.

Sarah and I passed the Charterston Clinic. One day a nurse at the clinic forced Doksi to drink castor oil. He didn't want to, but she threatened to wallop him with a hose-pipe.

Behind the clinic there was a grove of huge bluegum trees. It was dark ... very dark. A breeze made the leaves of the trees rustle. I

heard the sound of cars in the distance. They
were on the road that went far away. I also
heard lots of noise from the beerhall next to the
clinic. The men were drinking beer after work.
It was Friday night!

Then I felt Sarah's hand touch mine. Her fingers
closed tightly around my fist.

'It's so dark,' she said. 'You should protect me
when trouble comes.'

'Of course I'll protect you,' I said confidently. I really did want to look after her. But I was also afraid of ghosts. People said that ghosts sometimes lived in big trees. We picked our way carefully through the shadows.

Sarah held my hand more tightly. She tugged on my arm so that I had to stop. Then Sarah pulled me towards her. The leaves rustled. The noise from the beerhall scared me. It felt as if people were looking at us.

Sarah put her hands on my shoulders and held me at arm's length.

Although it was dark, I felt Sarah's eyes looking right into me. Then my throat began to hurt.

Sarah spoke. But her voice had changed. It was deep and scary. It made me think of Danger when it was cold outside and he howled to be let into the house.

'Have you ever kissed?' Sarah asked.

My throat hurt more than ever before. I remembered Miss Shezi and Teacher kissing in the bushes behind the school. Doksi and I threw stones at them. Then we ran away, shouting, 'We saw you!' And we laughed underneath our handkerchiefs.

'Mother kisses me in the mornings before I go to school,' I said.

Sarah laughed. 'I mean have you ever kissed a girl,' she insisted.

'Yes. Teboho kisses me sometimes.'

She laughed again. But my throat was hurting. Sarah's voice had changed. It made me think of Danger, when it was cold outside.

'No! What I mean is ... of course, you are still young,' she said.

'I know the two most important kinds of kisses,' I added boldly. 'They are the English kiss and the French kiss.'

'Hawu! This child is silly,' said Sarah.

Her words reminded me to say: 'I passed my exams.'

'That's good,' she replied. 'People say that you are clever.'

I smiled modestly in the dark. 'You passed too,' I returned her compliment. 'You are clever too!'

'Oho! Mfm! You make people laugh at me.'

Somehow I forgot about what the Bible said, because Sarah came closer. Closer. Our bosoms touched. Her hands crushed me. Sarah was powerful! When she embraced me, her rings pressed into my back. Sarah had many rings on her fingers.

My throat was very sore. Sarah began to moan

like Danger, when he howled to be let into the house. All this moaning scared me. Sarah was moving her hands all over my back. I thought she was mad. Then she began to breathe heavily. Sarah was hurting me. She was crushing me.

'*Sarah, what are you doing to me?*' It was that little voice again. I heard it inside my head, but it wouldn't come out of my mouth. '*Leave me alone, Sarah, or I'll tell Mother. You're crushing me. No! No!*'

I tried to push her away, but her hands were like webs. They moved all over my back. Sarah's breath was hot against my face. She kissed my eyes and my forehead. When she kissed my cheeks her lips made a popping sound. It was just like when *Gogo* kissed me.

'*Sarah is mad! Sarah is mad!*' the voice in my head repeated.

She gripped me as tightly as a policeman in town. I was frozen with fear. I whimpered.

'*Sarah, what are you doing to me?*'

Her mouth pressed against mine. Her tongue wiped my lips. Her breath was hot.

'Open your mouth! Open! Open!'

That was what Teacher said to Miss Shezi. I felt Sarah's tongue forcing its way between my lips. I had to let it in. There was silence. I almost began to enjoy myself ...

... But then Sarah moaned again. She shook her hips against my belly. Then I felt her fingers, her fingers covered with rings. They were mad fingers. Mad! They touched me everywhere.

I began to struggle again. Sarah's breath was hot against my face. It was hot. The leaves of the trees rustled. The noise from the beerhall made me scared. Sarah breathed in gasps.

'Sarah is mad! Sarah is mad! Sarah is mad!'

Sarah pushed me back until I bumped against a tree. She squashed me against the trunk. Sarah was moaning and gasping like a knock on the door.

'I'll shout! I'll tell Mother. What are you doing to me, Sarah? I'll shout!'

But my voice did not come out. My throat hurt when I tried to speak. Sarah's hips rubbed against my belly. My belly became hot. It was like when primitive men rubbed sticks together to make fire. Sarah clung to me fiercely, crushing me. Her breath was hot against my face.

'Sarah, you are killing me!'

Suddenly Sarah let out a long moan. She relaxed her grip on me.

I pushed her away and ran like the wind!

Sarah called after me. I ran towards
Mackenzieville, where the bioscope was. I ran
and ran and ran. Sarah's calls died away. I
passed the church. I heard people singing
inside, but I ran on. Then I couldn't hear Sarah
any more.

I didn't stop running until I reached
Mackenzieville. At last I felt a bit safer. The
bioscope was about to begin. People were filing
in like miners. I saw Tshidi and Doksi's brother
in the queue. They were holding hands.

Goodbye

I was still in bed the next morning, thinking
about Sarah and last night, when I heard a voice
I knew in the kitchen. 'I came to see you
yesterday evening, Teboho, but you were out.
Your brother told me that you might have gone
to church.'

It was Sarah!

I ran through to the kitchen. Sarah and I looked

at each other. Our eyes spoke. That was what
Teacher said to Miss Shezi in the bushes: 'Your
eyes are speaking to me.'

'You!' Sarah wagged her finger at me and
smiled. There was a big ring on that finger.
There were rings on all her fingers.

'Hha! What have I done?' I asked.

Teboho looked puzzled.

Sarah did not answer my question. In fact, she
did not even look at me again.

'I have come to say goodbye,' she said to
Teboho. 'I am going to stay in Durban. I have
just been waiting for the school to close.'

My sister was very surprised. And so was I.

'So Sarah's men will never take their revenge on me,' I thought. 'Never! She will never have the chance to tell them about yesterday.'

Before long Sarah left. I watched her go. I saw the deep hollows behind her knees. Sarah was beautiful. Sarah was leaving me ...

'I love you, Sarah!'

But my throat was dry and my voice did not come out.

Word List

abolished (page 4) - brought to an end
ambushed (page 8) - attacked unexpectedly
bellowed (page 8) - shouted loudly and angrily
bioscope (page 27) - place where films are shown
boldly (page 42) - bravely or strongly
brilliant (page 29) - very clever
clink (page 18) - knock together to make a sound
convertible (page 29) - kind of car with a roof that
    can be folded down
corporal punishment (page 4) - a caning or beating
embarrassment (page 31) - a feeling of shyness and
    foolishness
envied (page 4) - were jealous of; wanted to be like
fiercely (page 46) - very strongly with lots of feeling
filed (page 3) - walked one behind the other
grove (page 38) - small group of trees
grumble (page 9) - complain
Hygiene (page 34) - lessons about health and
    cleanliness
jeered (page 5) - laughed at; mocked
modestly (page 42) - shyly, humbly
nudged (page 6) - pushed gently
overjoyed (page 32) - very, very happy
pirate (page 26) - sea-robber

prefer (page 35) - like better

primitive (page 46) - savage, early in history

puzzled (page 48) - confused

resolution (page 3) - firm decision

shillings (page 38) - British coins used in South Africa before 1961; they were worth about ten cents

sneaked (page 35) - crept up quietly

sulking (page 13) - feeling unhappy and angry

threatened (page 10) - warned

took revenge on (page 1) - got even with

trembled (page 9) - shook slightly

wallop (page 38) - thrash; hit hard

whimpered (page 44) - cried softly

---

atjar (page 19) - hot pickles made from fruit or vegetables

Baba (page 31) - Father

Gogo (page 44) - granny

Heyi wena! (page 30) - Hey you!

Hhayi! (page 31) - No!

inyanga (page 38) - traditional doctor

magwinya (page 14) - deep-fried cakes, something like doughnuts; *vetkoek*

sjambok (page 21) - whip

Some facts about the writer

Njabulo Simakahle Ndebele grew up in Western Native Township in Johannesburg. Later he lived in Charterston Location in Nigel. This is where this story takes place.

Njabulo first wrote poetry. He wanted to use his writing to fight against the wrongs in society. When he was a student Njabulo began to write short stories. Njabulo has a number of university degrees. He is now the Vice-Chancellor and Principal of the University of the North.

Njabulo is one of South Africa's best known writers. He is the president of the Congress of South African Writers. *The Prophetess* is one of the stories in a book called *Fools and Other Stories* by Njabulo S. Ndebele. *Fools* won the Noma Award for Publishing in Africa in 1984.